Comes to This

Jeff Weddle

Nixes Mate Books
Allston, Massachusetts

Copyright © 2017 Jeff Weddle

Book design by d'Entremont
Cover photograph from the collection of Lauren Leja

All rights reserved. This book or any portion thereof may not be reproduced or used in any manner whatsoever without the express written permission of the publisher except for the use of brief quotations in a book review or scholarly journal.

Grateful acknowledgement is made to the following, where some of these poems previously appeared: *Chickenshit Bingo*; *Belinda Subramann's Gypsy Art Show*; *Chiron Review*; *Heavy Bear*; *Nihilistic Review*; *Nixes Mate Review*; *Pressure Press Presents*; *Ship of Fools*; *Waxing & Waning*; *The Wingnut Brigade*.

ISBN 978-0-692-86922-2

Nixes Mate Books
POBox 1179
Allston, MA 02134
nixesmate.pub/books

Always for Jill

After Everything Else Happened	1
Kindred	3
This Cool, Green Hour	6
Something about Harry	9
Bessie Carnie Weddle (1900 – 1984)	11
Writer's Block Faulkner	14
Will You Please Just Listen?	16
You Know Her	17
The One	18
The Light of the World	20
It was a Saturday	22
Tattoo	23
Another Couple	25
Comes to This	27
Glory	28
Yet We Seek	29
Flight	30
The Situation	30
Reckoning	34
Dance, God Damn It. Dance	35
See America First	38
Of Course	40
Miss America	42
Hunters on the Road	43
The Second Coming	46
Admit It	48

Comes to This

After Everything Else Happened

Sometime later the sky opened
things fell upon us
upon the streets and houses
upon the cars and movie theaters
upon the old women with canes
and their idiot husbands
sometime later the sky opened
things fell upon the bicycle riders
and acrobats
upon the prostitutes and police officers
upon the destitute and dying
and the beautiful girls with auburn hair
and the brave young men with flowers
things fell
crushing those objects you might imagine
they would crush
even dogs and children
not cats, of course,
for cats are wise and adept
at vanishing
but it was unspeakable
this crushing
so I can't comment on what they were

these things that fell upon us
that crushed us
but sometime later the sky opened
it did
and things fell upon us
and things fell
and fell
and fell
and I was not sad
because I knew it was coming
and I am, after all, a man
and I do not give in to sorrow
I will miss you, though
beautiful one
I will miss you most of all
I will miss you like my own blood
amid this wasted splendor

Kindred

you antichrist poets
and sad bombers
you trumpeters
you fish out of water
you sharks and aardvarks
you with your souls
in your hip pockets
and your hearts
in my head
you misbegotten
you clangers
of joyful noise
you malcontent
confectioners of
undiscovered mad
insouciant joy
you harbingers of delight
you fish heads and thieves
you dolts of pleasure
and genius desire
you crazies
you punks
you conquering heroes

you simple prophets
you philanderers
you hawkers of sex dreams
and spilled ambition
you with the burnt toast
spleen of regret
you who love devoured
you who know the stars' meaning
and the distance between heart
and hollow
you who are forever my brothers
and my sisters
you who are my loves
you who disregard my missed chances
you who offer books like bread
and words like roses
you who make me weep
you are the flesh of the storm
and the body of jitterbug gospel
and the map of all dimensions
and the lost tourist seeking direction
and the blessings and lights of the world

my hands in your hands
my blood in your veins

my children your children
my embrace forever

This Cool, Green Hour

days when air holds you
like an absent caress
and trees stand like answers
to unasked questions
days when your cat is more wise
than the Buddha
and your dog doesn't care
days when the coffee
in your favorite cup
tastes like joy
and smells like laughter
days when you
no longer feel old
and are braver, by far,
than Christ
days when the world
blossoms in your hands
and you can't even
give it away
days when children teach love
and whisper the secret destiny
of the world
days when all rivers flow true

and the stars know your meaning
days like this one
days when found paper scraps
hold more light than Shakespeare
days when your strength is certain
days when the mountains of childhood
are no longer vast
but you, finally, are
days like that
days like glazed donuts
and red wine
shared on the best afternoon in 1978
days like Key West and cold beer
days like a childhood friend
somehow returned and whole
and laughing
days like right this second
like this pen in my hand
like the world daring me to breathe
like a great rift in everything
like magic
days when I see
your smiling eyes

and know all the years are prologue
that you will hold me forever
and nothing ever
ever
ever
ends

Something about Harry

Harry brings his daughter
to the bus each morning
which takes her
I presume
to a special school.

There is something profoundly
wrong with her
and the burden must be crushing
but he has not given up.

Once Harry fell asleep
with the bathtub running
and flooded his whole house.
There were men over there for a week
with trucks and hoses
but he has not given up.

Most mornings as I drive
my children to school
I pass Harry out walking his dog.
His eyes never lift from the dog or the street
though he often waves to me

if I catch him standing in his yard.

In a few minutes
I'll go outside to get the paper
and there he'll be
escorting his daughter to the bus.
"Good morning neighbor,"
I'll say.
He'll wave.

A great man, unknown.

Time for coffee.

Bessie Carney Weddle (1900–1984)

She was dying
before the flood

and when the call came
the rescue squad
took us to the hospital
in a small, open boat.

My mother my father my grandfather me.

There's nothing wrong
with that old girl
my grandfather said.

He kept talking like that
as the tiny boat
chopped its way across
the floodwaters.

My father
kept saying
Mom's very sick.

But the old man, smiling and joking:
She's all right.

She was ten minutes gone
when we got there.

My grandfather
bent double
crying
we've lost
our best
friend.

The trip back was silent,
of course.

My mother
held the old man
in her arms
while my father cried
and I focused
on the slick, wet trees.

It was nothing
special, I guess:

just the remains
of a family, just
a boat cutting through
a flood.

Writer's block Faulkner

The Sound and the Fury just wasn't
coming together the way he'd hoped
and Faulkner was desperate.
Estelle had already blown the cash
he'd made from *Mosquitos* and *Soldier's Pay*
and the creditors were beating down his door.
He decided to call Hemingway.
"Hey Papa," he said. "Got any ideas
for this book I'm writing?"
So, Hemingway drove up from the Keys
and he and Faulkner got drunker than snakes,
and after Bill passed out,
Ernie dashed off a couple of hundred pages.
Faulkner read them when he woke up,
but couldn't make sense of anything.
He figured though, since it was Hemingway,
what the hell.
He published it verbatim in his own name.
That's when the critics began taking notice,
and Faulkner let Hemingway write
the rest of his books in exchange
for hot nights upstairs with Estelle –
Go Down, Moses, *Absalom*, and the rest –

and Faulkner came up with his plan
for the day Hemingway would squeal:
Manufactured insanity,
a small, backwater town,
and a double-barrel 12-gauge.
Everything was perfect.
All he had to do was accept the accolades,
act artsy,
and wait.

Will You Please Just Listen?

Precision above all
and no wasted words.
Do you understand the lesson?
At best, you will almost get there.
To the truth, I mean.
Scratch that.
Truth is for dopes.
We're not dopes, are we?
The difference between
the right word
and the almost right word
is a kick in the balls.
This is not a trap
though many
assume it to be.
Hold tight.
We are bound for glory
and I understand everything.

You Know Her

Beautiful girl has
no umbrella, she carries
her shoes in the rain.

She's a sonata
minor chords and broken glass
ashtrays, lies, spilled wine.

The One

He lusted for pretty girls
who never knew he breathed
the genius air
and slept on benches
when he was lucky
and that one night
when Satan and God
drank moonshine
till you couldn't tell
which was the meaner
it was he who found
them wasted in the streets
and blessed them
and made his bargains
to save the world.
They ripped out his soul
of course
and cast it on the winds.
Listen close
when the moon
swims high
and if you hear the voice
it means he is singing

maybe for you alone.
Cherish your luck.
He is our father
this poet that nobody knows.

The Light of the World

Paula knew how to write a poem.
Her words bit and held
and every line was better
than any line you could write.

Paula drank Jim Beam
straight from the bottle
and chased it with beer.

Paula sent her poems to the magazines
and the magazines said she was a miracle.

Paula ate pills until her hands shook
and she could barely move.

Paula read her poems in the bars
and the drunks hooted
and laughed and talked loudly
among themselves.

Paula tried to hang herself
in the living room

using a ceiling fan
and a leather dog leash.

Paula stopped reading in bars
and sending her poems to the magazines.

Paula fell off the porch
and broke her leg in three places,
lay writhing on the lawn
for a half hour until a neighbor
finally heard the screams.

Paula quit writing and works
in a factory making pre-packaged
breakfast food.

Paula danced with the gods
and the gods fucked her good.
But the magazines were right:
Paula was a blinding miracle.

Never heard of her? Isn't that
the way it works?

It was a Saturday

It was a Saturday and her hair,
somewhere between
wild and deadly,
and demanding touch,
demanding hungry fingers
to linger a moment
on her neck, the warm skin, sweat.
It was a Saturday
and she was a chameleon –
blonde, brunette,
but eyes always blue –
and that laugh....
It was a Saturday
and the night was heavy with autumn,
and even the stars stopped breathing.
Of course it was a Saturday.
A week, a month, a thousand years
make no difference.
Some days remain unfinished,
and Saturdays are the best.

Tattoo

Nobody knew Big Mike was dead
as Nadine sat there with her new tattoo,
a crimson heart,
and she twirled her hair
along the index finger of her right hand.
The tattoo was on her left shoulder,
and it was small,
and still smarted from the needle.
Nobody knew Big Mike was dead,
and the regulars drank their beer,
though it was flat and weak,
and they drank deliberate, slow, and sorry,
and waited for something to happen,
or nothing to happen,
and Nadine sat there waiting for something, too,
as the blood dried, and the flies circled,
and Big Mike was dead,
and the day was bright,
and in the streets some men destroyed worlds,
and some men begged for mercy,
and some just gave up,
while Nadine twisted her hair,
and Big Mike no longer cared

whether she would beg him to stay,
or just let him go,
and he would never see the tattoo
he had always wanted,
but never quite could convince her
to suffer.

Another Couple

He told Edna:

"Let's go find an old cafe in Paris, one the locals have mostly forgotten and the tourists never knew. We'll sit on the patio and drink. It will be absinthe to start, and we'll see where that takes us. Perhaps it will lead to opium in a small, dark apartment presided over by a thin Chinese man with a long mustache and longer braids, a man by the name of Loo. Before the night is over we're shanghaied and fighting pirates somewhere on the China Sea. Everything is held in the twisted knot of doom and romance. And the sky, always, is littered with stars. Let's go there."

Edna never stopped snoring.

He said:

"Let's go climb mountains and find the rare flowers that only grow on lost summits. Let's lure virgins into our bedroom and teach them all the pleasures. Let's rob banks and have shootouts with hero cops where somebody has to die."

Edna drooled on her pillow.

He said:

"Let me love you."

Edna farted and held tight to her dreams.

And he gave up
and slept
and the next day was like all the days.

And some nights he watched her sleeping
and as she wandered her own hidden dreams
he told the most marvelous secrets
and begged her to know him

even until his final breath.

And Edna, a faithful widow,
never tired of telling her friends
how he was kind and sweet
and a good provider

but oh, ladies, my God, ever so dull.

Comes to This

a second cup of coffee doesn't mean much
a dry muffin
a kitchen table with four chairs
and a man watching the squirrels play
through the window
everything quiet
everything quiet
a dog sleeps somewhere in the house
and a cat
and a wife
a second cup of coffee gets cold too soon
there are places to go
things to which he must attend
but he doesn't, just now, quite know how to stand
or the meaning of his flesh
his skin
the bones that cradle his heart
or what he might do
if he did

Glory

old cars are best
dusty roads leading
nowhere special
a girl in cut-offs
and blinding white tee
your arm around her shoulders
cold beer
sunshine   later stars
the broken face of the moon
you turn on the radio
and it plays songs
just for that moment
songs you won't ever hear again
in just that way
the world is dappled, twisting shadows
and nobody knows it better than you

Yet We Seek

There is a path, somewhere.
It is in a forest and I cannot say
there are places where it begins or ends
though it is absurd to think otherwise.
A path through the trees on the side of a mountain
a path with green all around
and chilled sunlight filtering through the leaves.
If I say, "Run child," will you listen?
If I say, "Step lightly"?
Of course you will not.
This path is not your path.
It waits for someone you wish you could be.
The only grace is knowing it is there.
You will never arrive, but this is why you wander.

Flight

All at once
we were flying.

She asked if we were angels.

I couldn't say.

"Only angels can do this,"
she whispered,
but I knew better about myself,
and figured the same for her.

Still, who knows?

Maybe we were big, magical birds,
or new creatures no one had seen before.

Maybe it was drugs we took and forgot,
or maybe we were airborne devils.

That's an explanation I could get behind.

And we were flying,
going higher and higher and higher.

I could see so far,
past mountain ranges and through rock walls
and to the bottom of the ocean.

I saw fantastic creatures living mundane lives,
and everywhere life, and death, and misery;
even fleeting joy.

Happiness.

And at last I looked into her heart,
and the radiance beggared understanding,
and blinded me,
and I fell,
kept falling,
as she sailed past the horizon.

Glory is wasted on the living and the dead don't care.

If you ever see her, pal, you'll know what I mean.

The Situation

These are the dire times
of great, wet mouths
and scorched promises.
Bloody teeth gnawing
on poor men's bones.

America, whom I have loved,
who has given light to my years,
is your light now finished?

These are the dire times.

The moon above us
does not blink,
but shames us with pure beauty.

Hungry children in their beds
will grow and live to ask
an accounting,
and by God by God by God
will be our best,
most impotent, reply.

These are the dire times.

Anger is all that's left us,
and night's cold blanket
is no comfort at all.

Reckoning

Everything is minor;
forget to put the groceries away
and the milk soon rots:
a kitchen filled with stink and vermin.
You find yourself alone,
a brown light hanging on the walls,
yesterday's shirt,
and the telephone rings
for no good reason.
There are young people
in the streets, laughing,
and you open the windows
to hear them better,
but it is no good.
Their laughter is only silence
raped by music.
The milk is bad and you pour it
down the sink. None of this is enough.
Soon, perhaps. These are small things.
We add them up and they tell us
what to do.

Dance, God Damn It. Dance

This is our hollow place.
This world that says a badge makes a hero,
that believes victims are thugs,
that does not remember Tina Modotti,
that has forgotten Emma Goldman,
this amnesiac, flattened landscape
of steadfast plastic and manufactured desire,
this Titanic an inch from hard ice,
this death rodeo,
this land that elevates trendy parasites to high office
and discards the truly good,
this nation that hated Eugene Debs
and murdered Joe Hill,
that extinguished Martin Luther King
on a Memphis balcony
and Medgar Evers in his home,
that blew Addie Mae Collins
and Denise McNair
and Carole Robertson
and Cynthia Wesley
to pieces,
that screams the name of Jesus
as it lets its children live in squalor

and praises God as they die in shame,
this blight, this cancer, this ugly scar.
This scab heaven.
This is our hollow place.
This is Orlando Charleston Sandy Hook
Aurora Boston Columbine Virginia Tech
Baton Rouge New York Vietnam Iraq
your house at the end of the lane.
This is headline and story.
This is Joe McCarthy and his questions.
This is earned darkness.
This is the sky breaking to blood.
This is tainted pleasure
and all the rotten eggs you can eat.
This is the March of history
and the revolution that never happened.
This is a monkey with a gun.
This is what they will allow.
This is what makes us happy.
This is music and liquid flesh.
This is the Hot 100 and the Host that Loves You Most.
This is the rule.
This is our hollow place.
This is pure sex and death.
This is the hood you wear.

This is your shackle.
This is what they give and what we take.
This is slow starvation.
This is our hollow place.
This is our war.
This is our 1930s dance marathon and no one wins.
This is tomorrow's bread line.
This is the unseen hand.
This is politics as usual,
the opium of the masses,
the murder of art,
the big win for the Gipper,
the girl you wouldn't give the time of day
and the heart inside her.
Remember your parents.
Remember the Mother Church and the Fatherland.
Remember the party.
Everything for the good of the party.
It is standard procedure.
It is our hollow place.
We know all of this, but we jump to the whip
with bright, shining faces.
This is our hollow place.
Remember your function:
Dance, God damn it. Dance.

See America First

I am sick like you're sick and I want to understand.
America, what have you done to us?
You are our pimp and pusher
and sainted church of Big Mac outrage
and sloganeered righteousness.
Air conditioned theaters with stadium seating
will only take you so far.
Reality television and pornography
will only take you so far.
Football and cold beer will only take you so far,
even if the home team crushes.
America, when did you become a fink?
When did you sell your body politic
to the dirty grease bags who want nothing more
than to rape your children – all of us –
in broad daylight and stinking alleys
and dirty apartments and swanky schools
and everywhere there is money to suck
or a soul blowing in an awkward, flag draped wind?
My country, 'tis of thee I write furtive letters
no one can ever read.
America, this isn't working out.
I think we should see other people, America.

It isn't me. It's you.
No, that's a lie.
We are in this together, America, and up to our eyeballs.
Oh, America. You bully.
You coward.
Blood is easy when it's across the world,
and the blood of the people here
is only a problem when we complain.
But we hate complainers, right America?
Pull yourself up by your bootstraps, by God,
and exercise your right to remain silent.
That's what you want, America.
I am sick in the same way you are sick.
I am dying and I see that I am dying.
I envy your naïveté, America.
Enjoy your slow and stupid death.

Of Course

parents love their children
and hard work pays off
and the man who bags
your groceries never
tortured a lost hitchhiker
in his basement
and buried what was left in his wall
after making a stew of her parts

and the police officers
patrolling you neighborhood
never murder for sport

and no one you know
goes to bed hungry
or bereft of love

and your wife would never fuck another

and America is number one
and Jesus loves you
and voting matters

and the teams you worship are the best teams
and most likely worship you back
and your church has the inside scoop
and you, yourself,
are good

and prosperity is right around the corner

and your lost darlings still think of you
and there was once a chance for joy
and you had a day, a single day
that was the best
and made all the other days worth living

and you will be remembered
in song and glory
though death
has forgotten your name

Miss America

I say she was intrepid,
alive for days in that basement,
clown mask tight on her face, bound and drugged.
What must have been her idyll?
The mind cannot take such force,
even when led into puddles of narcotic stupor,
even when every obscenity becomes common.
I say she was intrepid,
and when she wandered
into the unforgiving asphalt streets,
the concrete hive,
she might have been a saint.
The blood was not hers alone,
and she was a blade.
Do not forget.

Hunters on the Road

The cars look like any car
and the men look like
all the miserable souls you've ever imagined;

or they look like your insurance agent,
or your high school coach,
or your father,
or the president of the PTA,
or the guy who shingled your roof last year,
or a helpful librarian, an exterminator,
a chef, a fireman, a cop,

or they look like your minister,
your wife's cousin,
your trash collector,

or your mirror.

All across America they drive roads
where maybe your car has stalled
or perhaps your children are walking.

They are outside movie theaters,

and beside convenience stores,
and in mall parking lots.

They love mall parking lots.

These men will ask for your help,
or maybe offer assistance.

Maybe a ride to the nearest gas station
or a lift home,
or a good time on a lonely night.

And if you go with them
your night will be as lonely
as all the world's sorrow,

and those few who notice
will marvel at how you merged with absence,
and some may even feel the sting
of the small, ragged hole you left behind.

Remember this when you step out for a gallon of milk,
or exchange greetings with that friendly stranger,

or when you close your eyes tonight and dream.

There are hunters in this world and one of them has seen your face.

The Second Coming

He remembered
being dead
but only
for a second.
After that
he was
just a guy
driving down
a familiar street
in a car
he had owned
for six years
on his way
to pick up
his daughter
from gymnastics.

Being dead wasn't so bad
especially since
death mostly had the substance
of daydream.

All those souls he had devoured,
he didn't remember any of that.
Forgetting was his gift
and no one in the world
could reasonably accuse him
of anything.

He was just a guy in a six year old car
a guy with erectile dysfunction
a guy with a mortgage that was eating him alive
a guy with a daughter he adored
a daughter whose terminal cancer
was not yet detected

and a wife who drank too much
and sometimes fucked the neighbors.

Hell comes as hell comes.

It's all in the details.

Admit It

Every day, it's the same.
It's the same in the cities and in
small towns, in the cornfields and
coal mines. It's the same on trolley
cars and busses and space craft.
It's the same in the cabs of 18-wheelers
and the helms of ships.
Everywhere, men praying for death.
Men walking along the street –
your street – or running. Men in
suits, in prison garb, in dresses.
Men, everywhere, praying for death.
A quick death, a finality.
Not the lingering insult of cancer,
the sorrow of pain piling on right till the end,
but a quick exit. Say, a heart attack while
carrying groceries in from the car,
or a 3:00 a.m. burglar with a handgun
and wrecked nerves. He wants death, too.
Men with wives they have endured for decades.
Men with sunken eyes, sunken chests.
Men whose bodies have outlived their spirits
and men whose spirit is all that remains.

Men without women or with the wrong woman,
the very worst thing.
Men with nothing, men with the riches of kings,
everywhere, wanting to die.
Wanting it right this moment.
Praying for oblivion.
Say, sitting on a couch,
and watching a popular television show,
or talking on the telephone with their mother.
Maybe sitting in a yellow chair, elbows propped
upon a white table, a dim light
hanging from the ceiling.
Everything is an act of prayer,
like writing a poem,
or coming to the end of a page
and deciding just to stop.

About the Author

Jeff Weddle grew up in Prestonsburg, a small town in the hill country of Eastern Kentucky. He has worked as a public library director, disc jockey, newspaper reporter, Tae Kwon Do teacher, and fry cook, among other things. His first book, *Bohemian New Orleans: The Story of the Outsider and Loujon Press* (University Press of Mississippi, 2007), won the Eudora Welty Prize and helped inspire Wayne Ewing's documentary, *The Outsiders of New Orleans: Loujon Press* (Wayne Ewing Films, 2007), for which Weddle served as associate producer. His poems, stories, and essays have appeared in dozens of venues, including the anthologies *Surreal South '13* (Press 53, 2013); *Pressure Press Presents* (Pressure Press, 2014); *Stovepiper* (Stovepiper Books, 1994) and *Mondo Barbie* (St. Martin's Press, 1993). Weddle is the author of a poetry collection, *Betray the Invisible* (OEOCO, 2010), a limited-edition, fine press book handcrafted by master book artist Mary Ann Sampson, and a chapbook of Barbie poems, *Not Another Blonde Joke* (Implosion Press, 1991). He is an associate professor in the School of Library and Information Studies at the University of Alabama.

Nixes Mate is a tiny island in Boston Harbor first used by colonists to graze their sheep. The island became infamous after the bodies of convicted pirates were gibbetted there to serve as warnings to mutinous sailors.

Nixes Mate Books features small-batch artisanal literature, created by writers that use all 26 letters of the alphabet and then some, honing their craft the time-honored way: one line at a time.

Other Nixes Mate titles:
On Broad Sound | Rusty Barnes
Kinky Keeps the House Clean | Mari Deweese
Squall Line on the Horizon | Pris Campbell
Hitchhiking Beatitudes | Michael McInnis

Forthcoming titles from Nixes Mate Books:
Lubbock Electric | Anne Elezabeth Pluto
Nixes Mate Review Anthology 2016/17
Stories | Lauren Leja

nixesmate.pub/books

www.ingramcontent.com/pod-product-compliance
Lightning Source LLC
Chambersburg PA
CBHW051958290426
44110CB00015B/2295